Push and Pull
Understanding Force and Motion

Quinn Bitterman

ROSEN COMMON CORE READERS

Rosen Classroom™

New York

Published in 2014 by The Rosen Publishing Group, Inc.
29 East 21st Street, New York, NY 10010

Book Design: Jon D'Rozario

Photo Credits: Cover AVAVA/Shutterstock.com; p. 5 (both) Thomas Northcut/Thinkstock.com; p. 7 Jacek Chabraszewski/Shutterstock.com; p. 9 Fotokostic/Shutterstock.com; p. 11 Feng Yu/Shutterstock.com; p. 13 Warren Glodswain/Shutterstock.com; p. 15 gorillaimages/Shutterstock.com; p. 17 VALERY HACHE/AFP/Getty Images; p. 19 Stock Montage/Archive Photos/Getty Images; p. 21 (background) AISPIX/Shutterstock.com; p. 21 (basketball) Sonya Isherwood/Shutterstock.com; p. 21 (football) Amy Myers/Shutterstock.com; p. 21(sled) Andrew Lundquist/Shutterstock.com; p. 22 Bonita R. Cheshier/Shutterstock.com.

ISBN: 978-1-4777-2354-8
6-pack ISBN: 978-1-4777-2355-5

Manufactured in the United States of America

CPSIA Compliance Information: Batch #CS13RC: For further information contact Rosen Publishing, New York, New York at 1-800-237-9932.

Contents

What Are Forces?

When you wake up in the morning, you push your blanket off to get out of bed. When you go to bed at night, you pull your blanket over you to fall asleep. By pushing and pulling the blanket, you change its position and **location**. This change is called motion. The pushing or pulling that makes the motion happen is called force. We see examples of force all around us!

The force of a person pushing or pulling an object like a blanket is what causes it to move.

Down to Earth

Gravity is a force that causes any two objects in the universe to be drawn toward each other. The more mass an object has, the greater its gravity. It's what pulls us to Earth and keeps us from floating in the air. When we trip and fall to the ground, that's gravity at work!

Gravity is also the force that keeps Earth and other planets orbiting, or moving around, the sun.

When we jump in the air, the force of gravity brings us back to the ground.

Make It Move!

Applied force is another force we see around us every day. This kind of force exists when a person or object pushes or pulls something else. When you push a toy car across the floor, applied force is acting on the car.

Another example of applied force is a person moving a desk across a classroom. Applied force is what gives the desk its motion.

When you kick a soccer ball, you're using applied force to make the ball move.

Is It Normal?

When you put a heavy book on a table, what allows the table to hold the weight of the book? Why doesn't gravity pull the book to the ground?

A force called normal force is what keeps a thick book from moving through the table. The table pushes against the book, and this upward push is called normal force. This kind of force exists when one object touches another, **stable** object.

Normal force is what keeps this large book on the table. Sometimes it's hard to see normal force at work.

Feeling the Friction

One type of force happens when two **surfaces** touch each other. This is called friction. Friction works against motion between two surfaces. The force of friction usually moves in the **opposite** direction of the way an object is moving.

Friction is what keeps our feet from sliding over the ground. The ground pushes against our shoes, and we don't slip!

Ice cuts down on friction, which makes slipping possible.

One kind of friction is called air resistance. This force acts upon objects as they travel through the air. **Molecules** in the air slow things down because of friction.

We often don't notice air resistance. The only times it can really be felt are when objects move through the air very quickly. Air resistance is also noticed when the moving objects are very large.

If you ski, you can feel air resistance working against you as you move quickly down a hill.

Tension Force

Some forces only run through certain kinds of objects. Tension force only exists with a string, rope, or wire. When a piece of string is pulled tightly from opposite ends, you can see tension force in action. This force tugs the string equally in both directions. Tension force keeps the string **stretched** tightly.

You can see tension force at the circus! It's what keeps a tightrope stretched tightly so people can walk on it.

The Laws of Motion

Scientists have studied forces and motion throughout history. The most famous scientist is Sir Isaac Newton. He studied math and science in England. In 1687, he wrote about motion. He came up with three laws of motion, which taught people how force and motion work. Newton's three laws are so well known that we still use them today to discuss force and motion.

Scientists, teachers, and students continue to talk about and use Newton's three laws of motion hundreds of years after he wrote them.

Sir Isaac Newton

Newton's first law of motion states that an object or a body will either keep moving or stay at rest unless it's acted on by an outside force. His second law of motion says that a force can change the speed and direction of an object's motion. Newton's third law states that every force has an equal and opposite force.

It's easy to see Newton's three laws at work in the world around us.

Newton's Laws in Our World

First Law of Motion

A sled will keep moving down a hill unless an outside force stops its motion.

Second Law of Motion

When a football player is hit by another player, he slows down. His direction also changes as he falls to the ground.

Third Law of Motion

When you bounce a ball on the ground, the ball pushes against the ground, and then the ground pushes back, causing the ball to bounce back up.

All Around Us

Forces and motion are important parts of our lives. Forces work together and against one another in order to help us move through the world around us. The force of gravity keeps us from flying into the air. The force of friction keeps us from slipping when we walk. What ways do you see force and motion at work in the world around you?

Glossary

location (loh-KAY-shun) Where something is.

molecule (MAH-lih-kyool) The smallest part of something.

opposite (AH-puh-zuht) Being at the other end or side; as different as possible.

scientist (SY-uhn-tihst) Someone who studies the way things work and the way things are.

stable (STAY-buhl) Not moving or changing.

stretch (STREHCH) To pull tightly.

surface (SUHR-fuhs) The top part of something that can be seen.

Index